To

_____

From

_____

The love of God surrounds us
Like the air we breathe around us—
As near as a heartbeat,
As close as a prayer,
And whenever we need Him,
He'll always be there.

GOD'S PROMISES
FROM A TO Z

God's Promises
from A to Z

Helen Steiner Rice

Compiled by
Virgina J. Ruehlmann

Revell
a division of Baker Publishing Group
Grand Rapids, Michigan

© 1999 by Virginia J. Ruehlmann and Helen Steiner Rice Foundation Fund, LLC, a
wholly owned subsidiary of Cincinnati Museum Center. All rights reserved.

Published by Revell
a division of Baker Publishing Group
P.O. Box 6287, Grand Rapids, MI 49516-6287
www.revellbooks.com

New edition published 2011

Printed in China

Library of Congress Cataloging-in-Publication Data
Rice, Helen Steiner.
    God's promises from A to Z / Helen Steiner Rice ; compiled by Virginia J.
Ruehlmann. — New ed.
      p. cm.
    ISBN 978-0-8007-1955-5 (cloth)
    1. Christian poetry, American. 2. God (Christianity)—Promises—Poetry. I.
Ruehlmann, Virginia J. II. Title.
    PS3568.I28G645 2010
    811'.54—dc22
                                                   2010043855

11   12   13   14   15   16   17   7   6   5   4   3   2   1

$\mathcal{T}$o all who seek
the meaning, compassion, and glory
of God's promises
and grasp the value
and rippling effect
of one's own personal promises

INTRODUCTION

During the course of a lifetime, we make many promises. A promise might take many forms. A promise can be implied, written, signed, or sealed with a handshake. How long do promises remain? Some are nullified by mutual agreement or by the courts, and some are sustained by law. Some expire, and some last forever.

Theologians estimate that 30,000 to 36,000 of God's promises have been identified in the Bible. Approximately 7,500 of these were made by God to humankind. God's promises offer guidance for everyday conflicts, for all types of problems, and for salvation through Jesus Christ.

Helen Steiner Rice addressed in poetic form many of God's promises regarding the trials, tribulations, joys, and sorrows of life. In this book a number of God's promises are paired with poems by Mrs. Rice. As you read, allow these verses to bring cheer, comfort, peace, relief, and solace into your life.

SINCERELY,
VIRGINIA J. RUEHLMANN

ACCEPTANCE,
ADVERSITY

*T*his is the confidence we have in approaching God:
that if we ask anything according to his will, he
hears us. And if we know that he hears us—whatever we
ask—we know that we have what we asked of him.

1 JOHN 5:14–15 NIV

God in His goodness has promised
that the cross He gives us to wear
Will never exceed our endurance
or be more than our strength can bear.
And secure in that blessed assurance,
we can smile as we face tomorrow,
For God holds the key to the future,
and no sorrow or care we need borrow.

nd why are you anxious about clothing? Consider the lilies of the field, how they grow; they neither toil nor spin; yet I tell you, even Solomon in all his glory was not arrayed like one of these."

MATTHEW 6:28–29

Be of Good Cheer
There's Nothing to Fear

Cheerful thoughts like sunbeams lighten up the darkest fears,
For when the heart is happy there's just no time for tears,
And when the face is smiling it's impossible to frown,
And when you are high-spirited you cannot feel low-down.
For the nature of our attitudes toward circumstantial things
Determines our acceptance of the problems that life brings,
And since fear and dread and worry cannot help in any way,
It's much healthier and wiser to be cheerful every day.
And if you'll only try it, you will find, without a doubt,
A cheerful attitude's something no one should be without,
For when the heart is cheerful it cannot be filled with fear,
And without fear the way ahead seems more distinct and clear,
And we realize there's nothing that we must face alone,
For our heavenly Father loves us, and our problems are His own.

*A*re not two sparrows sold for a penny? And not one of them will fall to the ground without your Father's will. But even the hairs of your head are all numbered. Fear not, therefore; you are of more value than many sparrows."

MATTHEW 10:29–31

There Is a Reason for Everything

Our Father knows what's best for us, so why should we
  complain?
We always want the sunshine, but He knows there must be rain.
We love the sound of laughter and the merriment of cheer,
But our hearts would lose their tenderness if we never shed a tear.
Our Father tests us often with suffering and with sorrow;
He tests us not to punish us but to help us meet tomorrow.
For growing trees are strengthened when they withstand the
  storm,
And the sharp cut of a chisel gives the marble grace and form.
God never hurts us needlessly and He never wastes our pain,
For every loss He sends to us is followed by rich gain.
And when we count the blessings that God has so freely sent,
We will find no cause for murmuring and no time to lament.
For our Father loves His children and to Him all things are
  plain,
So He never sends us pleasure when the soul's deep need is pain.
So whenever we are troubled and when everything goes wrong,
It is just God working in us to make our spirits strong.

*H*ave no anxiety about anything, but in everything by prayer and supplication with thanksgiving let your requests be made known to God. And the peace of God, which passes all understanding, will keep your hearts and your minds in Christ Jesus.

PHILIPPIANS 4:6–7

Adversity Can Distress Us or Bless Us

The way we use adversity is strictly our own choice,
For in God's hands adversity can make the heart rejoice.
For everything God sends to us, no matter in what form,
Is sent with plan and purpose, for by the fierceness of a storm
The atmosphere is cleared and the earth is washed and clean,
And the high winds of adversity can make restless souls serene.
And while it's very difficult for mankind to understand
God's intentions and His purpose and the workings of His
   hand,
If we observe the miracles that happen every day,
We cannot help but be convinced that in His wondrous way
God makes what seemed unbearable and painful and
   distressing
Easily acceptable when we view it as a blessing.

BELIEFS,
BLESSINGS

*J*esus said to her, "Did I not tell you that if you would believe you would see the glory of God?"

JOHN 11:40

If we put our problems in God's hand,
There is nothing we need understand.
It is enough just to believe
That what we need we will receive.
The love of God is too great to conceive.
Don't try to explain it—just trust and believe!

And we know that in all things God works for the good of those who love him, who have been called according to his purpose.

ROMANS 8:28 NIV

There Are Blessings in Everything

Blessings come in many guises
That God alone in love devises,
And sickness, which we dread so much,
Can bring a very healing touch,
For often on the wings of pain,
The peace we sought before in vain
Will come to us with sweet surprise,
For God is merciful and wise.
And through long hours of tribulation
God gives us time for meditation,
So no sickness can be counted loss
That teaches us to bear our cross.

*A*gain I say to you, if two of you agree on earth about anything they ask, it will be done for them by my Father in heaven. For where two or three are gathered in my name, there am I in the midst of them."

MATTHEW 18:19–20

Look on the Sunny Side

There are always two sides—
   the good and the bad,
The dark and the light,
   the sad and the glad—
But in looking back over
   the good and the bad,
We're aware of the number
   of good things we've had,
And in counting our blessings,
   we find when we're through,
We've no reason at all
   to complain or be blue.

So thank God for the good things
     He has already done,
And be grateful to Him
     for the battles you've won,
And know that the same God
     who helped you before
Is ready and willing
     to help you once more.
Then with faith in your heart,
     reach out for God's hand
And accept what He sends,
     though you can't understand.
For our Father in heaven
     always knows what is best,
And if you trust His wisdom,
     your life will be blessed.
So always remember that
     whatever betide you,
You are never alone,
     for God is beside you.

COMFORT

*B*lessed be the God and Father of our Lord Jesus Christ, the Father of mercies and God of all comfort, who comforts us in all our affliction, so that we may be able to comfort those who are in any affliction, with the comfort with which we ourselves are comforted by God.

2 CORINTHIANS 1:3–4

There's a lot of comfort in the thought
  that sorrow, grief, and woe
Are sent into our lives sometimes
  to help our souls to grow . . .
For through the depths of sorrow
  comes understanding love,
And peace and truth and comfort
  are sent from God above.

It's Me Again, God

Remember me, God?
   I come every day
Just to talk with You, Lord,
   and to learn how to pray.
You make me feel welcome,
   You reach out Your hand.
I need never explain,
   for You understand.
I come to You frightened
   and burdened with care,
So lonely and lost
   and so filled with despair,
And suddenly, Lord,
   I'm no longer afraid—
My burden is lighter
   and the dark shadows fade.
Oh, God, what a comfort
   to know that You care
And to know when I seek You,
   You'll always be there.

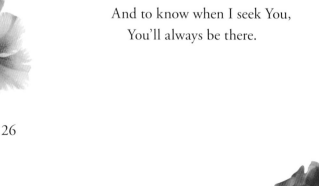

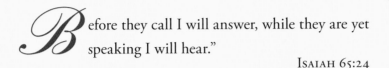

efore they call I will answer, while they are yet speaking I will hear."

ISAIAH 65:24

God Is Everywhere

Sometimes the things that seem the worst
    turn out to be the best,
So think of this as just a time
    to get a little rest.
And while we cannot understand
    why things happen as they do,
The One who hangs the rainbow out
    has His own plans for you.
And may it comfort you to know
    that you are in His care,
And God is always with you,
    for God is everywhere.

*N*ow may our Lord Jesus Christ himself, and God our Father, who loved us and gave us eternal comfort and good hope through grace, comfort your hearts and establish them in every good work and word.

2 Thessalonians 2:16–17

Part of the Plan

God did not promise sun without rain,
Light without darkness or joy without pain,
But He has promised strength for the day
When the darkness comes and we lose our way.
And when we seek shelter in His wondrous love
And ask Him to send us help from above,
Then we find comfort and know it is true
That bright, shining hours and dark, sad ones too
Are part of the plan God made for each one,
And all we need pray is "Thy will be done."

This, then, is how you should pray: 'Our Father in heaven, hallowed be your name, your kingdom come, your will be done on earth as it is in heaven. Give us today our daily bread. Forgive us our debts, as we also have forgiven our debtors. And lead us not into temptation, but deliver us from the evil one.' For if you forgive men when they sin against you, your heavenly Father will also forgive you."

MATTHEW 6:9–14 NIV

DISCOURAGEMENT, DOUBT

*T*hough I walk in the midst of trouble, thou dost preserve my life; thou dost stretch out thy hand against the wrath of my enemies, and thy right hand delivers me.

PSALM 138:7

It's easy to grow downhearted
　　when nothing goes your way.
It's easy to be discouraged
　　when you have a troublesome day.
But trouble is only a challenge
　　to spur you on to achieve
The best that God has to offer
　　if you have the faith to believe.

*H*umble yourselves therefore under the mighty hand of God, that in due time he may exalt you. Cast all your anxieties on him, for he cares about you.

1 PETER 5:6–7

God's Hand Is Always There

I am perplexed and often vexed
And sometimes I cry and sadly sigh,
But do not think, dear Father above,
That I question You or Your unfailing love.
It's just that sometimes when I reach out,
You seem to be nowhere about,
And while I'm sure You love me still
And I know in my heart that You always will,
Somehow I feel I cannot reach You,
And though I get on my knees and beseech You,
I cannot bring You close to me,
And I feel adrift on life's raging sea.
But though I cannot find Your hand
To lead me on to the promised land,
I still believe with all my being
Your hand is there beyond my seeing.

$\mathcal{A}$sk, and it will be given you; seek, and you will find; knock, and it will be opened to you. For every one who asks receives, and he who seeks finds, and to him who knocks it will be opened."

MATTHEW 7:7–8

Anxious Prayers

When we are deeply disturbed with a problem
    and our minds are filled with doubt,
And we struggle to find a solution
    but there seems to be no way out,
We futilely keep on trying
    to untangle our web of distress,
But our own little, puny efforts
    meet with very little success.
And finally, exhausted and weary,
    discouraged and downcast and low,
With no foreseeable answer
    and with no other place to go,
We kneel down in sheer desperation
    and slowly and stumblingly pray,
Then impatiently wait for an answer,
    which we fully expect right away.
And then when God does not answer
    in one sudden instant, we say,
"God does not seem to be listening,
    so why should we bother to pray?"
But God can't get through to the anxious,
    who are much too impatient to wait—
You have to believe in God's promise
    that He comes not too soon or too late.

Encouragement,
Eternal Life

I am the living bread which came down from heaven; if any one eats of this bread, he will live for ever; and the bread which I shall give for the life of the world is my flesh."

Life is eternal, the good Lord said,
So do not think of your loved one as dead.
For death is only a stepping-stone
To a beautiful life we have never known—
A place where God promised we would be
Eternally happy and safe and free,
A wonderful land where we live anew
When our journey on earth is over and through.

The Way of the Cross
Leads to God

He carried the cross to Calvary—
Carried its burden for you and me.
There on the cross He was crucified,
And because He suffered and bled and died,
We know that whatever our cross may be,
It leads to God and eternity.
For who can hope for a "crown of stars"
Unless it is earned with suffering and scars,
For how could we face the living Lord
And rightfully claim His promised reward
If we have not carried our cross of care
And tasted the cup of bitter despair?

Let those who yearn for the pleasures of life
And long to escape all suffering and strife
Rush recklessly on to an empty goal
With never a thought of the spirit and soul—
But if you are searching to find the way
To life everlasting and eternal day,
With faith in your heart take the path that He trod,
For the way of the cross is the way to God.

*J*esus said to her, "I am the resurrection and the life;
he who believes in me, though he die, yet shall he
live, and whoever lives and believes in me shall never die.
Do you believe this?"

JOHN 11:25–26

In Hours of Discouragement
God Is Our Encouragement

Sometimes we feel uncertain
 and unsure of everything—
Afraid to make decisions,
 dreading what the day will bring.
We keep wishing it were possible
 to dispel all fear and doubt
And to understand more readily
 just what life is all about.
God has given us the answers,
 which too often go unheeded,
But if we search His promises
 we'll find everything that's needed
To lift our faltering spirits
 and renew our courage too,
For there's absolutely nothing
 too much for God to do.
So cast your burden on Him,
 seek His counsel when distressed,
And go to Him for comfort
 when you're lonely and oppressed.
For God is our encouragement
 in troubles and in trials,
And in suffering and in sorrow
 He will turn our tears to smiles.

_W_hen you pass through the waters I will be with you; and through the rivers, they shall not overwhelm you; when you walk through fire you shall not be burned, and the flame shall not consume you."

Isaiah 43:2

FAITH

*I*s the law, therefore, opposed to the promises of God? Absolutely not! For if a law had been given that could impart life, then righteousness would certainly have come by the law.

GALATIANS 3:21 NIV

When everything is pleasant and bright
And the things we do turn out just right,
We feel without question that God is real,
For when we are happy, how good we feel.
But when the tides turn and gone is the song
And misfortune comes and our plans go wrong,
Doubt creeps in and we start to wonder,
And our thoughts about God are torn asunder—
For we feel deserted in times of deep stress
Without God's presence to assure us and bless.
And it is when our senses are reeling
We realize clearly it's faith and not feeling.

*N*o temptation has overtaken you that is not common to man. God is faithful, and he will not let you be tempted beyond your strength, but with the temptation will also provide the way of escape, that you may be able to endure it.

1 CORINTHIANS 10:13

Do You Believe?

When the way seems long and the day is dark
And we can't hear the song of the thrush or the lark,
And our hearts are heavy with worry and care,
And we are lost in the depths of despair,
That is the time when faith alone
Can lead us out of the dark unknown.
For faith to believe when the way is rough
And faith to hang on when the going is tough
Will never fail to pull us through
And bring us strength and comfort too.
For all we really ever need
Is faith as a grain of mustard seed,
For all God asks is do you believe—
For if you do you shall receive.

Thou dost keep him in perfect peace, whose mind is stayed on thee, because he trusts in thee.

Isaiah 26:3

Great Faith That Smiles
Is Born of Great Trials

It's easy to say "In God we trust"
   when life is radiant and fair,
But the test of faith is only found
   when there are burdens to bear.
For our claim to faith in the sunshine
   is really no faith at all,
For when roads are smooth and days are bright
   our need for God is so small.
And no one discovers the fullness
   or the greatness of God's love
Unless they have walked in the darkness
   with only a light from above.
For the faith to endure whatever comes
   is born of sorrow and trials
And strengthened only by discipline
   and nurtured by self-denials.
So be not disheartened by troubles,
   for trials are the building blocks
On which to erect a fortress of faith
   secure on God's ageless rocks.

Climb Till
Your Dream Comes True

Often your tasks will be many,
　　and more than you think you can do.
Often the road will be rugged,
　　and the hills insurmountable too.
But always remember the hills ahead
　　are never as steep as they seem,
And with faith in your heart, start upward
　　and climb till you reach your dream.
For nothing in life that is worthy
　　is ever too hard to achieve
If you have the courage to try it
　　and you have the faith to believe.
For faith is a force that is greater
　　than knowledge or power or skill,
And many defeats turn to triumphs
　　if you trust in God's wisdom and will.
For faith is a mover of mountains—
　　there's nothing that God cannot do—
So start out today with faith in your heart
　　and climb till your dream comes true.

J tell you the truth, if you have faith as small as a mustard seed, you can say to this mountain, 'Move from here to there' and it will move. Nothing will be impossible for you."

MATTHEW 17:20 NIV

GRACE

*T*hree times I pleaded with the Lord to take it away from me. But he said to me, "My grace is sufficient for you, for my power is made perfect in weakness." Therefore I will boast all the more gladly about my weaknesses, so that Christ's power may rest on me.

2 Corinthians 12:8–9 niv

God, be my resting place and my protection
In hours of trouble, defeat, and dejection.
May I never give way to self-pity and sorrow,
May I always be sure of a better tomorrow,
May I stand undaunted, come what may,
Secure in the knowledge I have only to pray
And ask my Creator and Father above
To keep me serene in His grace and His love.

For by grace you have been saved through faith; and this is not your own doing, it is the gift of God— not because of works, lest any man should boast.

EPHESIANS 2:8–9

Dark Shadows Fall
in the Lives of Us All

Sickness and sorrow come to us all,
But through it we grow and learn to stand tall,
For trouble is part and parcel of life,
And no one can grow without struggle and strife.
The more we endure with patience and grace,
The stronger we grow and the more we can face,
And the more we can face, the greater our love,
And with love in our hearts we are more conscious of
The pain and the sorrow in lives everywhere—
So it is through trouble that we learn to share.

He Loves You

It's amazing and incredible,
    but it's as true as it can be—
God loves and understands us all,
    and that means you and me.
His grace is all-sufficient
    for both the young and old,
For the lonely and the timid,
    for the brash and for the bold.
His love knows no exceptions,
    so never feel excluded—
No matter who or what you are,
    your name has been included.
And no matter what your past has been,
    trust God to understand,
And no matter what your problem is,
    just place it in His hand.
For in all of our unloveliness
    this great God loves us still—
He loved us since the world began,
    and, what's more, He always will!

*T*herefore, since we are justified by faith, we have peace with God through our Lord Jesus Christ. Through him we have obtained access to this grace in which we stand, and we rejoice in our hope of sharing the glory of God.

ROMANS 5:1–2

For the Lord God is a sun and shield; he bestows favor and honor. No good thing does the Lord withhold from those who walk uprightly. O Lord of hosts, blessed is the man who trusts in thee!

PSALM 84:11–12

Showers of Blessings

Each day there are showers of blessings
    sent from the Father above,
For God is a great, lavish giver,
    and there is no end to His love.
And His grace is more than sufficient,
    His mercy is boundless and deep,
And His infinite blessings are countless—
    and all this we're given to keep
If we but seek God and find Him
    and ask for a bounteous measure
Of this wholly immeasurable offering
    from God's inexhaustible treasure.
For no matter how big our dreams are,
    God's blessings are infinitely more,
For always God's giving is greater
    than what we are asking for.

HAPPINESS,
HOPE

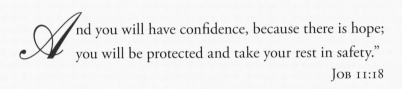

"And you will have confidence, because there is hope;
you will be protected and take your rest in safety."

JOB 11:18

The rainbow is God's promise
   of hope for you and me,
And though the clouds hang heavy
   and the sun we cannot see,
We know above the dark clouds
   that fill the stormy sky
Hope's rainbow will come shining through
   when the clouds have drifted by.

*F*or I know the plans I have for you, says the Lord, plans for welfare and not for evil, to give you a future and a hope. Then you will call upon me and come and pray to me, and I will hear you. You will seek me and find me; when you seek me with all your heart."

JEREMIAH 29:11–13

God Grant Us
Hope and Faith and Love

Hope for a world grown cynically cold,
Hungry for power and greedy for gold—
Faith to believe when, within and without,
There's a nameless fear in a world of doubt—
Love that is bigger than race or creed
To cover the world and fulfill each need . . .
God grant these gifts of faith, hope, and love—
Three things this world has so little of—
For only these gifts from our Father above
Can turn our hearts from hatred to love.

More Precious than Gold

Faith, hope, and love are more precious than gold,
For if you possess them, you've riches untold.
With faith to believe what your eyes cannot see
And hope to look forward to new joys to be
And love to transform the most commonplace
Into beauty and kindness and goodness and grace,
There's nothing too much to accomplish or do,
For faith, hope, and love will carry you through.

*L*et us hold fast the confession of our hope without wavering, for he who promised is faithful; and let us consider how to stir up one another to love and good works, not neglecting to meet together, as is the habit of some, but encouraging one another, and all the more as you see the Day drawing near.

HEBREWS 10:23–25

*B*ehold, we call those happy who were steadfast. You have heard of the steadfastness of Job, and you have seen the purpose of the Lord, how the Lord is compassionate and merciful.

JAMES 5:11

A Sure Way to a Happy Day

Happiness is something we create in our mind,
It's not something we search for and so seldom find.
It's just waking up and beginning the day
By counting our blessings and kneeling to pray.
It's giving up thoughts that breed discontent
And accepting what comes as a gift heaven-sent.
It's giving up wishing for things we have not
And making the best of whatever we've got.
It's knowing that life is determined for us
And pursuing our tasks without fret, fume, or fuss.
For it's by completing what God gives us to do
That we find real contentment and happiness too.

IDEALS

*I*f any one destroys God's temple, God will destroy him. For God's temple is holy, and that temple you are.

1 Corinthians 3:17

In this world of casual carelessness,
    it's discouraging to try
To keep our morals and our standards
    and our ideals high.
But no life is worth living
    unless it's built on truth,
And we lay our life's foundation
    in the golden years of youth.
So allow no one to stop you
    or hinder you from laying
A firm and strong foundation
    made of faith and love and praying.

Ideals Build a Nation

It only seems like yesterday
　　you were a little boy,
Cute and sweet and huggable,
　　your parents' pride and joy,
But now you are a young man
　　who has helplessly been hurled
Into the seething struggle
　　of a violent, changing world.
So remember as a member
　　of our younger generation—
It's your morals and ideals
　　that will help rebuild our nation.

For what will it profit a man, if he gains the whole world and forfeits his life? Or what shall a man give in return for his life? For the Son of man is to come with his angels in the glory of his Father, and then he will repay every man for what he has done."

MATTHEW 16:26–27

$\mathcal{J}$esus then said to the Jews who had believed in him, "If you continue in my word, you are truly my disciples, and you will know the truth, and the truth will make you free."

JOHN 8:31–32

Ideals Are like Stars

Remember that ideals are like
   stars up in the sky—
You can never really reach them,
   hanging in the heavens high,
But like the mighty mariner
   who sailed the storm-tossed sea
And used the stars to chart his course
   with skill and certainty,
You too can chart your course in life
   with high ideals and love,
For high ideals are like the stars
   that light the sky above—
You cannot ever reach them,
   but lift your heart up high
And your life will be as shining
   as the stars up in the sky.

JOY

For the kingdom of God is not food and drink
but righteousness and peace and joy in the Holy
Spirit; he who thus serves Christ is acceptable to God and
approved by men. Let us then pursue what makes for peace
and for mutual upbuilding.

ROMANS 14:17–19

God bless you most abundantly
with joys that never cease,
The joy of knowing that He came
to bring the whole world peace.

*B*ut for you who fear my name the sun of righteousness shall rise, with healing in its wings. You shall go forth leaping like calves from the stall."

MALACHI 4:2

Expectation! Anticipation! Realization!

God gives us a power we so seldom employ,
For we're so unaware it is filled with such joy.
The gift that God gives us is anticipation,
Which we can fulfill with sincere expectation,
For there's power in belief when we think we will find
Joy for the heart and peace for the mind.
And believing the day will bring a surprise
Is not only pleasant but surprisingly wise,
For we open the door to let joy walk through
When we learn to expect the best and most too,
And believing we'll find a happy surprise
Makes reality out of a fancied surmise.

KINDNESS

*A*nd he took a child, and put him in the midst of them; and taking him in his arms, he said to them, "Whoever receives one such child in my name receives me; and whoever receives me, receives not me but him who sent me."

MARK 9:36–37

In this busy world it's refreshing to find
People who still have the time to be kind,
People still ready—by thought, word, or deed—
To reach out a hand in the hour of need,
People who still have the faith to believe
That the more you give, the more you receive.

In His Footsteps

When someone does a kindness, it always seems to me
That's the way God up in heaven would like us all to be.
For when we bring some pleasure to another human heart,
We have followed in His footsteps and we've had a little part
In serving Him who loves us—for I'm very sure it's true
That in serving those around us, we serve and please Him too.

*A*nd whoever gives to one of these little ones even a cup of cold water because he is a disciple, truly, I say to you, he shall not lose his reward."

Matthew 10:42

LOVE

If I have the gift of prophecy and can fathom all
mysteries and all knowledge, and if I have a faith
that can move mountains, but have not love, I am nothing.
1 CORINTHIANS 13:2 NIV

Love is unselfish, understanding, and kind,
For it sees with its heart and not with its mind.
Love is the answer that everyone seeks.
Love is the language that every heart speaks.
Love can't be bought—it is priceless and free.
Love, like pure magic, is a sweet mystery.

Love One Another
As I Have Loved You

To love one another as God loved you
May seem impossible to do,
But if you will try to have faith and believe,
There's no end to the joy that you will receive.
For love works in ways that are wondrous and strange,
And there's nothing in life that love cannot change—
For love is the key that throws open the door
To the heart that was locked and lonely before.
Love is the answer to all the heart seeks,
And love is the channel through which God speaks—
And all He has promised can only come true
When you love one another the way He loved you.

You have heard that it was said, 'You shall love your neighbor and hate your enemy.' But I say to you, Love your enemies and pray for those who persecute you, so that you may be sons of your Father who is in heaven; for he makes his sun rise on the evil and on the good, and sends rain on the just and on the unjust."

MATTHEW 5:43–45

*J*esus answered him, "If a man loves me, he will keep my word, and my Father will love him, and we will come to him and make our home with him."

JOHN 14:23

What Is Love?

What is love? No words can define it—
It's something so great only God could design it.
It grows through the years in sunshine and rain,
In gladness and sadness, in pleasure and pain.
It's ever enduring and patient and kind—
It judges all things with the heart, not the mind.
And love can transform the most commonplace
Into beauty and splendor and sweetness and grace,
For love is unselfish, giving more than it takes,
And no matter what happens, love never forsakes.
It's faithful and trusting and always believing,
Guileless and honest and never deceiving.
Yes, love is beyond what we can define,
For love is immortal, and God's gift is divine.

MOTHERHOOD

Train a child in the way he should go, and when he is old he will not turn from it.

PROVERBS 22:6 NIV

It takes a mother's patience to bring a child up right—
Her courage and her cheerfulness to make a dark day bright.
It takes a mother's wisdom to recognize our needs
And to give us reassurance by her loving words and deeds.
And that is why, in all this world, there could not be another
Who could fulfill God's purpose as completely as a mother.

*H*onor your father and your mother, so that you may live long in the land the Lord your God is giving you."

Exodus 20:12 NIV

A Mother's Love Is a Haven in the Storms of Life

A mother's love is like an island
    in life's ocean vast and wide—
A peaceful, quiet shelter
    from the restless, rising tide.
A mother's love is like a fortress,
    and we seek protection there
When the waves of tribulation
    seem to drown us in despair.
A mother's love is like a tower
    rising far above the crowd,
And her smile is like the sunshine
    breaking through a threatening cloud.
A mother's love is like a beacon
    burning bright with faith and prayer,
And through the changing scenes of life
    we can find a haven there.
For a mother's love is fashioned
    after God's enduring love—
It is endless and unfailing
    like the love of Him above.

*C*hildren, obey your parents in the Lord, for this is right. "Honor your father and mother" (this is the first commandment with a promise), "that it may be well with you and that you may live long on the earth."

EPHESIANS 6:1–3

A Mother's Love

A mother's love is something
    that no one can explain—
It is made of deep devotion
    and of sacrifice and pain.
It is endless and unselfish
    and enduring, come what may,
For nothing can destroy it
    or take that love away.
It is patient and forgiving
    when all others are forsaking,
And it never fails or falters
    even though the heart is breaking.
It believes beyond believing
    when the world around condemns,
And it glows with all the beauty
    of the rarest, brightest gems.
It is far beyond defining,
    it defies all explanation,
And it still remains a secret
    like the mysteries of creation—
A many-splendored miracle
    we cannot understand
And another wondrous evidence
    of God's tender, guiding hand.

NEEDS

*J*esus replied: " 'Love the Lord your God with all your heart and with all your soul and with all your mind.' This is the first and greatest commandment. And the second is like it: 'Love your neighbor as yourself.' "

MATTHEW 22:37–39 NIV

From one year to another God will gladly give
To everyone who seeks Him and tries each day to live
A little bit more closely to God and to each other,
Seeing everyone who passes as a neighbor, friend, or brother,
Not only joy and happiness but the faith to meet each trial
Not with fear and trepidation but with an inner smile.

O taste and see that the Lord is good! Happy is the man who takes refuge in him! O fear the Lord, you his saints, for those who fear him have no want!

PSALM 34:8–9

No Favor Do I Seek Today

I come not to ask, to plead or implore You—
I just come to tell You how much I adore You,
For to kneel in Your presence makes me feel blessed,
For I know that You know all my needs best,
And it fills me with joy just to linger with You,
As my soul You replenish and my heart You renew,
For prayer is much more than just asking for things—
It's the peace and contentment that quietness brings.
So thank You again for Your mercy and love
And for making me heir to Your kingdom above.

Call to me and I will answer you, and tell you great and hidden things which you have not known."

Beyond Our Asking

More than hearts can imagine
    or minds comprehend,
God's bountiful gifts
    are ours without end—
We ask for a cupful
    when the vast sea is ours,
We pick a small rosebud
    from a garden of flowers,
We reach for a sunbeam
    but the sun still abides,
We draw one short breath
    but there's air on all sides.
Whatever we ask for
    falls short of God's giving,

For His greatness exceeds
    every facet of living,
And always God's ready
    and eager and willing
To pour out His mercy,
    completely fulfilling
All of our needs
    for peace, joy, and rest,
For God gives His children
    whatever is best.
Just give Him a chance
    to open His treasures,
And He'll fill your life
    with unfathomable pleasures.

OBEDIENCE

*B*ut this command I gave them, 'Obey my voice, and I will be your God, and you shall be my people; and walk in all the way that I command you, that it may be well with you.'"

JEREMIAH 7:23

Great is our gladness to serve God through others,
For our Father taught us we all are sisters and brothers,
And the people we meet on life's thoroughfares
Are burdened with trouble and sorrow and cares,
And this is the chance we are given each day
To witness for God and to learn to obey.

*N*ow therefore amend your ways and your doings, and obey the voice of the Lord your God, and the Lord will repent of the evil which he has pronounced against you."

JEREMIAH 26:13

"Thou Shalt Not Steal"

We glance at the commandments and read them through,
And then unthinkingly we say, "These things we never do."
But take, for example, "Thou shalt not steal."
Can you honestly say and truthfully feel
That in some small, unimportant way
You don't steal a little every day?
You pilfer time when you should be working
And look for excuses to camouflage shirking.
You covet things that your neighbor owns
And secretly envy his luck unbeknownst,
And then in your many unthinking ways
You rob God of reverence every day,
And then you boast and proudly say,
"Here's one commandment that I obey,"
When in some veiled and hidden way
You break this commandment most every day.

Peace,
Prayer

*P*eace I leave with you; my peace I give to you; not as the world gives do I give to you. Let not your hearts be troubled, neither let them be afraid."

JOHN 14:27

God placed the peace He promised into the hands of man,
But man has never kept that peace since endless time began,
For we have never understood, either now or then,
That peace comes not through battles but doing good to men.
And when we meet with strangers along life's thoroughfares,
Be not forgetful that thereby we pass angels unawares,
And when we are at peace with God, then only we will find
The peace on earth He promised and eternal peace of mind.

$\mathcal{F}$inally, brethren, farewell. Mend your ways, heed my appeal, agree with one another, live in peace, and the God of love and peace will be with you.

2 CORINTHIANS 13:11

If

If we but had the eyes to see
   God's face in every cloud,
If we but had the ears to hear
   His voice above the crowd,
If we could feel His gentle touch
   in every springtime breeze
And find a haven in His arms
   'neath sheltering, leafy trees,
If we could just lift up our hearts
   like flowers to the sun
And trust His Easter promise
   and pray, "Thy will be done,"
We'd find the peace we're seeking,
   the kind no man can give—
The peace that comes from knowing
   He died so we might live!

Daily Prayers Are Heaven's Stairs

The stairway rises heaven-high, the steps are dark and steep.
In weariness we climb them as we stumble, fall, and weep.
And many times we falter along the path of prayer,
Wondering if You hear us and if You really care.
Oh, give us some assurance, restore our faith anew,
So we can keep on climbing the stairs of prayer to You,
For we are weak and wavering, uncertain and unsure,
And only meeting You in prayer can help us to endure
All life's trials and troubles, its sickness, pain, and sorrow
And give us strength and courage to face and meet tomorrow.

$\mathcal{T}$ruly, truly, I say to you, if you ask anything of the Father, he will give it to you in my name."

JOHN 16:23

Whatever you ask in my name, I will do it, that the Father may be glorified in the Son; if you ask anything in my name, I will do it."

JOHN 14:13–14

Prayers Can't Be Answered Unless They Are Prayed

Games can't be won unless they are played,
And prayers can't be answered unless they are prayed.
So no matter how busy or crowded your day,
Make it a practice to take time to pray,
And never start wondering if God heard your prayer
Or if He is able to take care of your care.
But instead of a crown He sends us a cross,
And instead of rich gains we are made poor by loss.
But great is our gladness and rich our reward
If we trust the judgment and will of the Lord.

QUESTIONS

*T*he Lord is with you when you are with him. If
you seek him, he will be found by you, but if you
forsake him, he will forsake you."

2 CHRONICLES 15:2 NIV

In this restless world of struggle it is often hard to find
Answers to the questions that disturb our peace of mind,
But the answer to all living, God holds safely in His keeping—
Only when we know Him will we find what we are seeking.
And to know Him is to love Him, and to love Him is to find
The answer to all questions that fill every troubled mind.

And from his fullness have we all received, grace upon grace. For the law was given through Moses; grace and truth came through Jesus Christ.

JOHN 1:16–17

"In Him We Live, and Move, and Have Our Being"

We walk in a world that is strange and unknown,
And in the midst of the crowd we still feel alone.
We question our purpose, our part, and our place
In this vast land of mystery suspended in space.
We probe and explore and try hard to explain
The tumult of thoughts that our minds entertain,
But all of our problems and complex explanations
Of our inner feelings and fears and frustrations
Still leave us engulfed in the mystery of life
With all of its struggles and suffering and strife,
Unable to fathom what tomorrow will bring,
But there is one truth to which we can cling—
For while life's a mystery we can't understand,
The great Giver of life is holding our hand,
And safe in His care there is no need for seeing,
"For in Him we live, and move, and have our being."

RESURRECTION

*F*or God so loved the world that he gave his one and only Son, that whoever believes in him shall not perish but have eternal life."

JOHN 3:16 NIV

The sleeping earth awakens, the robins start to sing—
The flowers open wide their eyes to tell us it is spring.
The bleakness of the winter is melted by the sun—
The tree that looked so stark and dead becomes a living one.
These miracles of Easter, wrought with divine perfection,
Are the blessed reassurance of our Savior's resurrection.

And if the Spirit of him who raised Jesus from the dead is living in you, he who raised Christ from the dead will also give life to your mortal bodies through his Spirit, who lives in you.

ROMANS 8:11 NIV

I Know That
My Redeemer Liveth

All across the waking earth,
    great nature with perfection
Retells the Easter story
    of death and resurrection—
So trust God's all-wise wisdom
    and doubt our Father never,
For in the kingdom of our Lord
    there is nothing lost forever.

Life Is Forever
Death Is a Dream

If we did not go to sleep at night,
We'd never awaken to see the light—
And the joy of watching a new day break
Or meeting the dawn by some quiet lake
Would never be ours unless we slept
While God and all His angels kept
A vigil through this little death
That's over with the morning's breath.
And death, too, is a time of sleeping,
For those who die are in God's keeping,
And there's a sunrise for each soul—
For life, not death, is God's promised goal.
So trust God's promise and doubt Him never,
For only through death can man live forever.

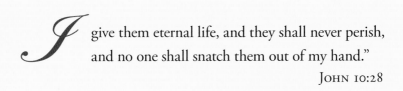

I give them eternal life, and they shall never perish,
and no one shall snatch them out of my hand."

JOHN 10:28

$\mathcal{T}$ruly, truly, I say to you, unless a grain of wheat falls into the earth and dies, it remains alone; but if it dies, it bears much fruit."

JOHN 12:24

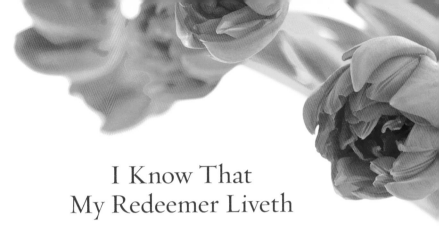

I Know That
My Redeemer Liveth

They asked me how I know it's true
    that the Savior lived and died
And if I believe the story
    that the Lord was crucified.
And I have so many answers
    to prove His Holy Being—
Answers that are everywhere
    within the realm of seeing—
The leaves that fall in autumn
    and were buried in the sod
Now budding on the tree boughs
    to lift their arms to God,
The flowers that were covered
    and entombed beneath the snow
Pushing through the darkness
    to bid the spring hello.
On every side, great nature
    retells the Easter story,
So who am I to question
    the resurrection glory?

Salvation,
Service

When Jesus spoke again to the people, he said, "I am the light of the world. Whoever follows me will never walk in darkness, but will have the light of life."

JOHN 8:12 NIV

The Lord is our salvation
    and our strength in every fight,
Our redeemer and protector,
    our eternal guiding light.
He has promised to sustain us,
    He's our refuge from all harms,
And He holds us all securely
    in His everlasting arms.

*I*f any one serves me, he must follow me; and where I am, there shall my servant be also; if any one serves me, the Father will honor him."

Show Me More Clearly the Way to Serve and Love You More Each Day

God, help me in my feeble way
To somehow do something each day
To show You that I love You best
And that my faith will stand each test,
And let me serve You every day
And feel You near me when I pray.
Oh, hear my prayer, dear God above,
And make me worthy of Your love.

The Home Beyond

We feel so sad when those we love
Are called to live in the home above.
But why should we grieve when they say good-bye
And go to dwell in a cloudless sky?
For they have but gone to prepare the way,
And we'll meet them again some happy day,
For God has told us that nothing can sever
A life He created to live on forever.
So let God's promise soften our sorrow
And give us new strength for a brighter tomorrow.

I write these things to you who believe in the name of the Son of God so that you may know that you have eternal life. This is the confidence we have in approaching God: that if we ask anything according to his will, he hears us.

1 JOHN 5:13–14 NIV

Everyone Needs Someone

People need people and friends need friends,
And we all need love, for a full life depends
Not on vast riches or great acclaim,
Not on success or worldly fame,
But on just knowing that someone cares
And holds us close in their thoughts and prayers,
For only the knowledge that we're understood
Makes everyday living feel wonderfully good.
And we rob ourselves of life's greatest need
When we lock up our hearts and fail to heed
The outstretched hand reaching to find
A kindred spirit whose heart and mind
Are lonely and longing to somehow share
Our joys and sorrows and to make us aware
That life's completeness and richness depend
On the things we share with our loved ones and friends.

*A*nd he sat down and called the twelve; and he said
to them, "If any one would be first, he must be last
of all and servant of all."

MARK 9:35

THANKFULNESS,
TRUST

*L*ook at the birds of the air: they neither sow nor reap nor gather into barns, and yet your heavenly Father feeds them. Are you not of more value than they?"

MATTHEW 6:26

Whatever our problems, troubles, and sorrows,
If we trust in the Lord, there'll be brighter tomorrows.
So keep on believing, whatever betide you,
Knowing that God will be with you to guide you,
And all that He promised will be yours to receive
If you trust Him completely and always believe.

*T*rust in the Lord with all your heart, and do not rely on your own insight. In all your ways acknowledge him, and he will make straight your paths.

PROVERBS 3:5–6

When Trouble Comes
and Things Go Wrong

Let us go quietly to God
    when troubles come to us.
Let us never stop to whimper
    or complain or fret or fuss.
Let us hide our thorns in roses
    and our sighs in golden song
And our crosses in a crown of smiles
    whenever things go wrong.
For no one can really help us
    as our troubles we bemoan,
For comfort, help, and inner peace
    must come from God alone.
So do not tell your neighbor,
    your companion, or your friend
In the hope that they can help you
    bring your troubles to an end,
For they too have their problems—
    they are burdened just like you—
So take your cross to Jesus,
    and He will see you through.

Meet Life's Trials with Smiles

There are times when life overwhelms us
    and our trials seem too many to bear—
It is then we should stop to remember
    God is standing by ready to share
The uncertain hours that confront us
    and fill us with fear and despair,
For God in His goodness has promised
    that the cross He gives us to wear
Will never exceed our endurance
    or be more than our strength can bear.

Endure hardship with us like a good soldier of Christ Jesus. No one serving as a soldier gets involved in civilian affairs—he wants to please his commanding officer.

2 TIMOTHY 2:3–4 NIV

*A*nd this is the testimony: God has given us eternal life, and this life is in his Son.

1 JOHN 5:11 NIV

Give Thanks Every Hour

We all have many things
    to be deeply thankful for,
But God's everlasting promise
    of life forevermore
Is a reason for thanksgiving
    every hour of the day
As we walk toward eternal life
    along the King's highway.

UNDERSTANDING

God said to [Solomon], "Because you have asked this, and have not asked for yourself long life or riches or the life of your enemies, but have asked for yourself understanding to discern what is right, behold, I now do according to your word. Behold, I give you a wise and discerning mind, so that none like you has been before you and none like you shall arise after you."

1 KINGS 3:11–12

Among the great and glorious gifts our heavenly Father sends
Is the gift of understanding that we find in loving friends,
For it's not money or gifts or material things,
But understanding and the joy it brings,
That can change this old world in wonderful ways
And put goodness and mercy back in our days.

For the Lord gives wisdom, and from his mouth come knowledge and understanding. He holds victory in store for the upright, he is a shield to those whose walk is blameless, for he guards the course of the just and protects the way of his faithful ones.

PROVERBS 2:6–8 NIV

A Personal Prayer

Bless us, heavenly Father—forgive our erring ways.
Grant us strength to serve Thee, put purpose in our days.
Give us understanding, enough to make us kind,
So we may judge all people with our hearts and not our minds.
And teach us to be patient in everything we do,
Content to trust Your wisdom and to follow after You.
And help us when we falter and hear us when we pray,
And receive us in Thy kingdom to dwell with Thee some day.

This is my prayer that I faithfully say
To help me to meet the new dawning day,
For I never could meet life's daily demands
Unless I was sure He was holding my hand.
And priceless indeed would be my reward
To know that you shared my prayer to the Lord.

Help Us to See and Understand

God, give us wider vision
   to see and understand
That both the sunshine and the showers
   are gifts from Thy great hand.
And when our lives are overcast
   with trouble and with care,
Give us faith to see beyond
   the dark clouds of despair.
And give us strength to rise above
   the mist of doubt and fear
And recognize the hidden smile
   behind each burning tear.
And teach us that it takes the showers
   to make the flowers grow,
And only in the storms of life
   when the winds of trouble blow

Can we too reach maturity
   and grow in faith and grace
And gain the strength and courage
   to enable us to face
Sunny days as well as rain,
   high peaks as well as low,
Knowing that the April showers
   will make May flowers grow.
And then at last may we accept
   the sunshine and the showers,
Confident it takes them both
   to make salvation ours.

My purpose is that they may be encouraged in heart and united in love, so that they may have the full riches of complete understanding, in order that they may know the mystery of God, namely, Christ, in whom are hidden all the treasures of wisdom and knowledge.

COLOSSIANS 2:2–3 NIV

135

VICTORY

I have fought the good fight, I have finished the race, I have kept the faith. Henceforth there is laid up for me the crown of righteousness, which the Lord, the righteous judge, will award to me on that Day, and not only to me but also to all who have loved his appearing.

2 TIMOTHY 4:7–8

When you're troubled and worried and sick at heart
And your plans are upset and your world falls apart,
Remember God's ready and waiting to share
The burden you find too heavy to bear.
So with faith, let go and let God lead the way
Into a brighter and less troubled day.

*F*or we ourselves were once foolish, disobedient, led astray, slaves to various passions and pleasures, . . . but when the goodness and loving kindness of God our Savior appeared, he saved us . . . in virtue of his own mercy.

Titus 3:3–7

Pattern for Living

More than poems to be read
    just for pastime and pleasure—
Here's a pattern for living
    to follow and treasure,
A wonderful program
    to practice each day
That will brighten your life
    and make easy your way.
For while it's been said
    that God's holy laws
Today are outmoded
    and musty with flaws,
Let no one entice you
    with new values or rules
Fashioned by renegades
    and practiced by fools,
For a full happy life
    and a lasting reward
Can only be gained
    through the laws of the Lord.

WISDOM,
WORRY

*D*aniel said: "Blessed be the name of God for ever and ever, to whom belong wisdom and might. He changes times and seasons; he removes kings and sets up kings; he gives wisdom to the wise and knowledge to those who have understanding."

DANIEL 2:20–21

The years go by and, as they do,
They only pause to smile on you,
For you hold together in happy thought
All the richness that this life has brought,
And you give so freely to all you meet
The wisdom that makes your life complete—
And you'll never grow old for you've so much to give,
And you'll always be young for you've learned how to live.

And God gave Solomon wisdom and understanding beyond measure, and largeness of mind like the sand on the seashore, so that Solomon's wisdom surpassed the wisdom of all the people of the east, and all the wisdom of Egypt.

1 KINGS 4:29–30

What Is a Birthday?

A birthday is a gateway
    between old years and new,
Just an opening to the future
    where we get a wider view—
Every year brings new dimensions
    that enable us to see
All things within a kinder light
    and more perceptively.
So birthdays are the gateway
    to what the future holds
And to greater understanding
    as the story of life unfolds.

In the day of prosperity be joyful, and in the day of adversity consider; God has made the one as well as the other, so that many may not find out anything that will be after him.

ECCLESIASTES 7:14

Talk It Over with God

You're worried and troubled about everything,
Wondering and fearing what tomorrow will bring.
You long to tell someone, for you feel so alone,
But your friends are all burdened with cares of their own.
There is only one place and only one Friend
Who is never too busy, and you can always depend
On Him to be waiting, with arms open wide,
To hear all the troubles you came to confide.
For the heavenly Father will always be there
When you seek Him and find Him at the altar of prayer.

Easier Grows the Way

Looking ahead, the hills seem steep
    and the road rises up to the sky,
But as we near them and start to climb,
    they never seem half as high.
And thinking of work and trouble,
    we worry and hesitate,
But just as soon as we tackle the job,
    the burden becomes less great.
So never a hill, a task, or load,
    a minute, an hour, a day,
But as we grow near it and start to climb,
    easier grows the way.

*Y*our word is a lamp to my feet and a light for my
path. I have taken an oath and confirmed it, that I
will follow your righteous laws.

Psalm 119:105–6 niv

X Symbol for
Christ

I am the gate; whoever enters through me will be saved. . . . I have come that they may have life, and have it to the full."

JOHN 10:9–10 NIV

Long, long ago in a land far away,
There came the dawn of the first Christmas Day,
And each year we see the promise reborn
That God gave the world on that first Christmas morn,
When the angels sang of peace on earth
And told men of the Christ child's birth.
For Christmas is more than a beautiful story—
It's the promise of life and eternal glory.

*W*hoever has my commands and obeys them, he is the one who loves me. He who loves me will be loved by my Father, and I too will love him and show myself to him."

JOHN 14:21 NIV

What Is Christmas?

Is it just a day at the end of the year—
A season of joy, merrymaking, and cheer?
Is it people and presents and glittering trees?
Ah no, it is more than any of these,
For under the tinsel and hidden from sight
Is the promise and meaning of that first Christmas
   night,
When the shepherds stood in wondered awe
And felt transformed by what they saw.
So let us not in our search for pleasure
Forego our right to this priceless treasure,
For Christmas is still a God-given day,
And let us remember to keep it that way.

YOUTH

*R*ejoice, O young man, in your youth, and let your heart cheer you in the days of your youth; walk in the ways of your heart and the sight of your eyes. But know that for all these things God will bring you into judgment.

ECCLESIASTES 11:9

You can't hold back the dawn,
 or stop the tides from flowing,
Or keep a rose from withering,
 or still a wind that's blowing.
And time cannot be halted
 in its swift and endless flight,
For age is sure to follow
 like day comes after night.
For He who sets our span of years
 and watches from above,
Replaces youth and beauty
 with peace and truth and love.

A Teenager's Prayer

God, here I am in a chaotic state,
Seeking some way to do something great.
I want to be someone who contributes to make
A less violent world for everyone's sake.
But whom can I go to and whom can I trust?
Who'll show me the difference between love and lust?
I'm willing to listen, I'm willing to do
Whatever it takes to make this world new,
But in the confusion and noise all around,
Where can the answer to my question be found?
Dear God, up in heaven, hear a teenager's plea—
Show me somehow what You want me to be.

I will instruct you and teach you in the way you should go; I will counsel you and watch over you.

PSALM 32:8 NIV

ZEAL

*H*e gives power to the faint, and to him who has no might he increases strength. . . . They who wait for the Lord shall renew their strength, they shall mount up with wings like eagles, they shall run and not be weary, they shall walk and not faint.

Isaiah 40:29, 31–32

God's commandments are advice especially for youth,
A pattern for living for all seekers of truth.
And you'll find that to follow these guideposts each day
Is not only the righteous and straight, narrow way
But a joyous experience, for there's many a thrill
In going God's way and in doing His will.

*N*ow who is there to harm you if you are zealous for what is right? But even if you do suffer for righteousness' sake, you will be blessed.

1 Peter 3:13–14

God, Give Us Drive but Keep Us from Being Driven

There's a difference between drive and driven—
The one is selfish, the other God-given—
For the driven man has but one goal,
Just worldly wealth and not riches of soul.
Ambition and wealth become his great needs
As daily he's driven by avarice and greed.
But most blessed are they who use their drive
To work with zeal so all may survive,
For while they forfeit great personal gain,
Their work and their zeal are never in vain
For they contribute to the whole human race,
And we cannot survive without growing in grace.
So help us, dear God, to choose between
The driving forces that rule our routine
So we may make our purpose and goal
Not power and wealth but the growth of our souls.
And give us strength and drive and desire
To raise our standards and ethics higher,
So all of us and not just a few
May live on earth as You want us to.

157

*N*ever flag in zeal, be aglow with the Spirit, serve the Lord. Rejoice in your hope, be patient in tribulation, be constant in prayer.

Romans 12:11–12

A New Sense of God

I find that all that was once possible for me to do with joyful eagerness and bubbling enthusiasm has somehow become more difficult. These days I find that the greatest source of comfort and inner peace and the only thing that can lift us above our earthly bondage is the deep sense of aloneness with God—which is not loneliness—for we only find true spiritual communion when we are alone and can have direct communication with God.